Out of the Boardroom and Into the Pasture

A Little Lesson About Leading with Love

Nigel Davidoff

*This book is dedicated to
Ken Nair, my main Tim*

1	In the Boardroom	1
2	Defending the Domain	4
3	Learning Love	7
4	What Love Isn't	12
5	It's Okay to Quit	20
6	Receiving Responses	25
7	Reviewing Responses	33
8	Penetrating Policies	39
9	Modifying Meetings	45
10	Repairing Reviews	52
11	Getting Started	61
12	Must We Lead with Love?	64
13	Into the Pasture	66
14	Step 0 – Humility	69
15	Step 1 – Mission	73
16	Step 2 – Discerning	76
17	Step 3 – Understanding	78
18	Step 4 – Awareness	82
19	Step 5 – Focus	87
20	Step 6 – Measure	91
21	*When the Mission is Misplaced*	96
22	*When Fear Pops Up*	100
23	*When the Executions Begin*	104
24	*When the Temperature Rises*	107
25	*Recognizing the Ultimate Leader in the Pasture*	111

Am I a Sheep?

It's basic zoology; people are not sheep.

We can call them sheep. We can treat them like sheep. But they're not sheep. People are people. Sheep are sheep.

Okay, that's out of the way. So why does it matter? We're about to explore the idea that the words chief, executive, and officer are poor words to describe a loving leadership model in today's business, church, and family organizations. In its place, we're going to look at the idea of a shepherd in the leadership role. However, when we do this, there's a risk: you might think I'm calling people sheep. I am not.

Churches have a well-accepted name for the person who is in the top leadership role; they call such person a pastor. This just confuses matters more. Most pastors don't 'pastor' – that is, most pastors do not shepherd. Most pastors execute, in the role of the official president of their organization. This sounds more like traditional CEO than shepherd.

Those who do some shepherding often see their constituents as sheep: a bunch of dumb animals with no hope for survival, if not for the intelligent, enlightened leader who can tell them where to go (and what to think as they go there).

But people are not sheep.

How do we describe an idea when the words we want to use have been misappropriated? I know of no other solution than to redefine them, through explanation and analogy. So that's what we're about to do – embark on a journey of re-thinking the ideas of organizational leadership, redefining goals, words, and ideas along the way.

I'm glad you're along for the ride!

Part 1

The Story of Advanced Minified
Technologies

Chapter 1

In the Boardroom

"Let's look at the numbers," Archie opened the monthly board meeting with an invitation to assess their present position.

Gail was up first, sitting directly to Archie's right. As the director of human resources, her official title was *Chief People Officer*. People was a much warmer term than human, and no human at Advanced Minified Technologies really wanted to be referred to as a resource. Gail did a good job embracing a new people-friendly language within their organization. 'Meetings' had become 'encounters' and 'reports' were translated as 'dispatches'. What she hadn't yet understood was the reality of new names for the same old thing. The new names might prompt people to stop and take a second look – but once they saw the substance behind the label, they realized they were still delivering the same old reports in the same old meetings.

Archie and Gail were in perfect unity on one idea: theirs would not be an old-fashioned, traditional, by-the-numbers company. It would be a modern, compassionate, people-focused organization. They believed in leading with love, and truly wanted the ideas of love and goodness to define their organization. But both had received their MBAs from the same time-honored institute of learning, and neither had ever lived outside of the traditional box. Swapping labels was the best they knew to do, and they both thought it was a bit revolutionary.

"Production is up 11% year-over-year," Gail read from the 'dispatch' she had prepared for this very important board 'encounter'. "But labor costs are up 39%."

Hunter jumped in. "Our labor cost gap has increased at every meeting I've been a part of. All of your grand ideas of a revolutionary business led by love is not going to work if you can't pay the rent."

This was not new information to Archie or Gail, nor to anyone else at AMT. They were confronted with the brutal reality: business is business, and business is first about the bottom line.

"Thanks Hunter, but I haven't got to the good news yet," Gail proclaimed. Gail was nothing if not consistent – always delivering the bad news up-front and finishing on a good note to encourage and inspire.

"Our new training initiative has improved efficiency across the company. The new wage laws and healthcare situation had us on track for a 42% increase in labor cost, but we reduced it to 39%. Our plan is working. We need to double-down on the training initiative in the next quarter. Not only is it loving and kind, but it's profitable."

Tim stroked his beard and looked toward the ceiling. Everyone knew what this meant. It was time to be quiet. Tim was a man of few words, but each word was full of wisdom. All eyes turned to him in eager anticipation.

"I don't think we love our people."

With that, Tim had contributed all he planned to say in that month's meeting.

Chapter 2

Defending the Domain

"That's a provocative statement," Archie was ready to defend the organization he led. "Gail's training initiative is helping everyone perform at a higher level. And the fact that we've kept everyone at their current health insurance levels despite rising costs is a clear example that we care about them. The rising minimum wage is entirely outside of our control, and I think we should focus on solutions to the real problems in front of us."

"I agree with Archie," Gail added. "Let's also not forget that Archie is giving up a lot of his valuable time for our *Dine with the Director* program, each week awarding someone a free lunch with the CEO. That shows people we care about them."

Simon sat to Archie's left. As the company's director of strategy, he and Gail had settled on *Chief Game Planner* as his title on the org chart. Simon always thought first and spoke later. He had been thinking since Tim threw out his bomb.

"Can we take five minutes to whiteboard all the loving things we do for our people?" Simon got up and walked to the whiteboard assuming an agreeable response. He knew most of the board members felt strongly that AMT was the most loving organization they were involved with.

As predicted, nobody tried to stop him. They were all eager to show the ways they expressed a kind and courteous work environment.

The board members each offered the initiatives and resolutions they were aware of, or had been a part of. After a few minutes, Simon had a solid and impressive list:

- *Maintain current insurance levels*
- *Always pay above the legal minimum*
- *Executives interact freely with employees*
- *Casual dress day*
- *The company party with an open bar (in quarters where key metrics had been exceeded)*
- *Paid paternity leave*
- *Extra maternity leave*
- *Lunchroom vending machines are set to half of retail prices*
- *Aggressive training*
- *401k matching*

"Good list, gang," Simon put the marker down. "These are all great things, and they make this a great place to work. But why do we do all these things?"

Although Simon was first a strategist, he had been exploring emotional intelligence in his own training, and knew that a little probing often revealed the motivations beneath the surface of a matter.

Archie was always about *the why*, and all eyes turned to him. Without much thinking, he expressed precisely why they did them. "This is how we express love to our employees. We lead with love."

Simon dug deeper. "What would happen if we stopped doing all these things tomorrow?"

Archie knew exactly what would happen. "Many of our employees would leave."

Gail agreed. So did the other board members, as indicated by their emphatic nods.

Simon posed the most interesting question of the meeting; in the second-most interesting sentence, "Is it possible we are motivated not so much by love, but by a fear of losing people?"

Tim's fingers went to his beard again. "I know that perfect love casts out all fear."

Chapter 3

Learning Love

"I'm not ready to buy that idea quite yet, Simon," Archie offered. "But I've been around long enough to know that sometimes we don't see our motivations without examining them. Let's put the quarterly reports on the back burner for a moment. None of those really matter if we're doing things for the wrong reasons, anyhow. Why don't you tell us more about this?"

Simon was unprepared. He had thrown out an idea, but didn't know what to do with it. He remembered one of Archie's favorite sayings: 'None of us is as smart as all of us.'

He picked up the marker again and cleared the whiteboard. "I think we all need to speak freely, and get rid of any defensiveness we have for the things we think we've done right. If you guys have any ideas, I'll write them down and we can discuss them. Tim, can you give us a good starting point?"

Everyone waited while Tim looked at the ceiling. A moment

passed, then another. Tim was by far the most accomplished member of their group. At 48 years old, he'd already created and sold four successful companies and written two best-selling books. Most people were astounded that a man who seemed to think so slowly could get so much done.

"We are an organization committed to loving our people," Tim finally spoke. "So what *isn't* love?"

"Um, I'm not sure what to write," Simon was slightly confused.

"Hate," offered Hunter.

"Hold on," Gail interrupted before Simon wrote anything. "In our new training, they're teaching us to look at ideas for what they aren't, which helps us clarify what they are. For example, you know in that spiritual class where they had us write down what God isn't?"

Those who had been a part of this remembered it vividly. It started out with the idea of what God is, and someone offered that God is our Father. The instructor wrote "God is NOT our father," and went on to explain that we cannot project the image of our flawed dads onto God, and that realization is a key step in understanding who or what God really is.

"So," Gail continued, "let's go with Tim's idea. Let's talk about what love isn't." She walked a few steps to the south end of the room where a framed poster of a Bible passage hung on the wall, and took it down. "This is I Corinthians 13, the minister read it at my wedding to exemplify what love is. Can we look at this together to discover what love isn't?"

She set the frame in the center of the boardroom table. Those close to it read from it, while others looked up the famous prose on their mobile phones, tablets, and laptops. They began to offer *isn't* ideas, while Simon wrote them on the whiteboard. He wrote small, realizing they used many different words for similar ideas.

✗	jealous	✗	quarrelsome
✗	boastful	✗	embittered
✗	arrogant	✗	sore
✗	rude	✗	disgruntled
✗	insists on its own way	✗	cynical
✗	irritable	✗	scornful
✗	resentful	✗	caustic
✗	rejoicing at wrong	✗	sarcastic
✗	giving up	✗	exasperating
✗	forceful	✗	irritating
✗	complaining	✗	grating
✗	impatient	✗	enraging
✗	protesting	✗	provoking
✗	inconsiderate	✗	burdensome
✗	uncaring	✗	bothersome
✗	inattentive	✗	nagging

✗	*thoughtless*	✗	*nitpicking*
✗	*uncivil*	✗	*defeating*
✗	*bad mannered*	✗	*distrusting*
✗	*unhelpful*	✗	*doubting*
✗	*malicious*	✗	*mistrusting*
✗	*malevolent*	✗	*suspecting*
✗	*mean*	✗	*disputing*
✗	*spiteful*	✗	*disbelieving*
✗	*crabby*	✗	*dismissive*
✗	*cranky*	✗	*rejecting*
✗	*grouchy*	✗	*spurning*
✗	*grumpy*	✗	*contesting*
✗	*petulant*	✗	*combative*
✗	*snarky*	✗	*eluding*
✗	*ornery*	✗	*evading*

Simon ran out of whiteboard. "Okay, I think that's enough. Anything else is probably some obscure word with the same meaning as something we've already written. This gives us enough to go on."

The room sat back and looked at the list.

Archie was the first to speak. "If that's what love isn't, I have to agree with Tim. I don't think we love our people."

Chapter 4

What Love Isn't

"I wonder if there's more to Simon's question than I'd like to admit," Archie pondered aloud. "What if our deepest motivation is not really leading with love, but is a desire for people not to quit?"

Archie had stumbled on one of the most dramatic truths in the whole world. While selfish motivations can have the same apparent outcome as loving motivations, they have an entirely different spirit and energy. Motivations were a key.

Archie's mind drifted back to last Valentine's Day and his big faux pas. He'd gone to the store and asked the shopkeeper for the largest box of heart-shaped chocolates in stock. The shopkeeper walked him over to a special case on the end cap of the Valentine's card and candy aisle. The top shelf of the case supported the most ornate velvet-wrapped heart-shaped box he'd ever seen. Around the perimeter of the heart were small crystals. The label revealed that inside the box were decadent single-source chocolates infused with a very pricey cognac. It was the only such box in the shop, and at $249.95 it was not the one most people went for.

"The fellow who buys that for his beau is certainly an impressive gentleman," the shopkeeper asserted.

"Sold!" declared Archie.

On the drive home, he called his best friend James. "You're not going to believe what I just bought Martha!" He went on to describe the box and the candy it contained. James was even more impressed than the shopkeeper.

On the 14th of February, Archie's last conference call went long, and the deadline was approaching for a Powerpoint he'd been working on. He spent extra time on it. He hadn't realized how late it was until Gail popped in to say goodbye. 'Oh no!' Archie thought, 'I promised Martha I'd be home at 5:30 and it's already 5:45!' He sent her a quick text message as he shut down his computer: "Running late. Sorry! XOXO"

At 6:15 Archie pulled in to his driveway, eager to see the look on Martha's face when he presented her with the chocolates.

He ran into the house, greeting Martha with a customary kiss, and held up a finger indicating 'hold on a second', while he skipped to his closet to retrieve the box. Hiding it behind his back, he walked out to Martha.

"I love you honey," he smiled as he offered her the radiant box. "Happy Valentine's Day!"

Martha accepted and held the box. The corners of her mouth turned down and a tear formed in the corner of her eye.

"Amazing, isn't it!" Archie effused.

Martha paused. Of course it was amazing. But it didn't make her feel loved. Not at all.

"Archie, do you remember when we took that Five Love Languages class?" Martha inquired.

Archie nodded in the affirmative.

"And do you remember our love languages, the ones we discovered through the class?" Martha continued questioning.

"I do. Yours was quality time and mine was acts of service."

"I remember it, too," Martha proceeded. "And I thought about what sort of act of service I could do to show you love today. I left work early and went to that butcher shop on Central and asked him for the nicest porterhouse steak he could cut. I made your favorite dinner of steak and rosemary roast potatoes. While it was cooking, I took to shining all your shoes, then reorganized your ties just the way you like them. I had dinner on the table at 5:30 with our best china. Fifteen minutes later, just before you texted, I put it all away in the fridge. I spent the next half hour awaiting your arrival and thinking about how to bring this up to you. I'm going to take a bath and soak for a while and, Archie, I'd like you to think about love and your motivations." She was not caustic, but was direct. She left the box on the table and headed to the master suite to start her bath.

Archie was stunned. His mind was racing.

He didn't feel right about eating the steak alone, so he grabbed a slice of cold pizza from the fridge and went out to the patio, where he did his best thinking.

'Quality time,' he thought. 'I gave my quality time to Powerpoint and conference calls today. Martha got what was left over, and it wasn't what I'd promised her. Not only did I not give her extra quality time on this special day, I gave her even less than I'd committed to. In fact, the idea of making extra time for Martha today hadn't even crossed my mind.'

Archie thought about how he could do a better job of prioritizing his schedule and showing Martha love through quality time. But his thoughts were constantly interrupted with the feeling of pride he'd experienced when the shopkeeper and his friend James congratulated him on his selection of Valentine's chocolates.

'Oh no!' Archie surprised himself with a sudden epiphany. 'The perceptions that James and that shopkeeper had of me were huge motivators in my choice of what to do for Martha on Valentine's Day. Once I'd received their affirmation, I stopped looking at Martha's needs and marinated in the confidence that I was the world's best husband. I didn't even stop to think about Martha's needs – only how she would see me when I revealed her gift.'

Archie sobbed about his newly discovered arrogance. He lamented the realization that he was first motivated with what made him feel good and right, and that he rarely took time to consider Martha's needs or feelings.

He was eager to apologize to Martha, but stopped himself. 'What if I'm apologizing primarily to make her think better of me?' he wondered. Of course, an apology isn't a bad thing, but if it comes from the wrong motivations, it's no better than the box of chocolates. He held himself in this uncertain place for a little longer.

After five more minutes had passed, he picked up his phone and sent an email to his assistant. "I'm leaving at 3:00pm every day next week," he typed. "If there's anything on my schedule for the late afternoon, please reschedule it to an available slot." Next he texted the babysitter, "We're going to need someone to watch the kids from 5-9 every day next week. Are you available?"

He put the phone back in his pocket and went inside. Instead of walking into his room as he usually did, he knocked on the door and waited. He'd already been enough of a relational bully with Martha today. His remorse and new perspective caused him to think of her first.

"Come in," Martha invited with a note of melancholy. She had finished her bath and was sitting in her chair in the corner of the room. She had a blanket over her legs, the one she liked to use when she prayed. Archie hadn't realized it, but almost an hour had passed on the patio.

Archie entered the room and sat on the bed across from Martha, his eyes level with hers. "Martha," he started, "first of all, thank you. Thank you for seeing in me what I refused to see in myself. Thank you for being an advocate for our marriage, and for being clear in helping me understand how to meet your needs. Second, I want to let you know that I have cleared every evening from my schedule next week, for time with you. Whatever you want to do is fine with me, whether it's going out for dinner or sitting at home, or even going to those classes you talked about at church. Next week, each evening, my time is all yours."

Martha glowed. "You know, Archie, I love you deeply. I couldn't help but notice that you didn't say you were sorry."

Archie jumped in, "Oops, well, I am. Very sorry."

Archie didn't yet realize, but he was still eager to have Martha think well of him, and used defensiveness to look good rather than listening intently to her heart. His apology was a defense.

"Stop, Archie. You didn't need to say sorry. I was going to tell you how happy it made me that you didn't. For years you've been saying sorry and not doing anything to fix your messes. In fact, you've taught me to lose hope every time you say sorry. Today is different – you didn't say sorry, you actually did something to show me that you're sorry. I would rather have 'show' than 'tell' any day of the week. Thank you, Archie. I love you. But please, don't make this a Valentine's Day thing – make it a shift in our marriage. It needs it."

With that, they embraced – longer than Archie was comfortable with, but as long as Martha needed.

"How about a do-over on dinner?" Martha asked as she stood up and headed toward the microwave.

That Valentine's Day they dined on slightly rubbery reheated steak and potatoes, followed by a more-than-healthy quantity of cognac-fill chocolates.

Martha threw the empty velvet box into the trash compactor and Archie pressed the start button. While it whirred, Martha stepped around Archie, facing him, and gave her beloved husband a glorious Valentine's Day kiss.

Chapter 5

It's Okay to Quit

"I think we need to take a new approach, because of our past motivations," Archie stated. "We must resolve to act in love, and if someone quits, that's okay."

Okay to quit? This didn't go over well, especially with Gail. "Archie, we need to focus on employee retention. We invest a lot into training our people, and the cost of replacing someone is enormous. We can't just have everyone quitting. We'll go bankrupt."

"You're right Gail," Archie agreed, "And lord knows I don't want anyone to quit. However, if the fear of someone quitting is driving this organization, and we're now embarking on truly leading with love, we have to be willing to have someone quit and take that out of the equation for now. We can reintroduce retention within the context of loving leadership, but outside of it, I think it's going to be a cancer to our company."

Although Archie wasn't always emotionally aware, he recognized the importance of addressing fear when it surfaced. He had learned to discern motivations, and while he didn't always do it in the moment, once he saw something he went for it.

"Gail, I think there is an undercurrent in our company. Our people hear us say we lead with love, but then they feel like we keep a stranglehold on them. I wonder if they don't stay because they feel loved, but because they're afraid to quit. This undercurrent of fear can never bring about the full, rich experience that we want all our team members to have."

Hunter jumped in, "I don't think fear is all bad. I think it can be a strong motivator for people, keeping them on track and doing the right thing. Also, what's wrong with doing good things so they fear leaving? It sounds like a win-win to me – we get to keep them around, and they get to enjoy a good work environment."

Simon had been thinking about this love versus fear thing since he had offered up the possibility that they were motivated by fear. "Hunter, you are absolutely correct," he confirmed. "Fear can be a strong motivator, and it works well a lot of the time. However, in our company, we have two problems with it. The first is keeping with our mission. We say that we are a loving company, and love and fear are poor bedfellows. If we're truly going to be the loving company we talk about, we have to spot fear and avoid giving it the steering wheel in our decisions. It's a matter of staying in integrity with our mission. Second, I think fear is a second-rate motivator. While it can work, it's not the best thing to motivate with. We want to be a great company, and to do so we have to eliminate the second-rate things that get in the way of the best things. I think we've come to rely on fear because it works, and that has kept us from going after the better way to motivate people."

This reminded Archie of his Valentine's Day motivations. He had been motivated, for sure, but the wrong reasons led him to be more hurtful than helpful toward the most important person in his life.

"I agree with Simon," Archie added to the conversation. "Fear works, but it's not AMT. Now that we've identified it, let's keep a close eye on fear and see where it pops up."

Gail's thoughts were whizzing as this conversation went on. "Team," she revealed, "every one of our policies seems to have a component that is fear based. Now that I look at things this way, I can see how we have a fear of losing people written into everything. For example, as a part of our expanded training initiative, we ask people to sign a statement of intent to stay with the company for at least six more months – before we'll send them for advanced training. And our paternity and maternity leave policies heavily penalize a parent who does not return to work immediately when their extended leave ends. When someone resigns, the first item on our checklist requires us to address whether they are aware they won't likely get the same health insurance benefits anywhere else. I think all of these, at their deepest level, are motivated by a fear of people quitting."

"That's good information," Archie thanked her. "And I want to make sure we're clear – none of those things are bad in and of themselves. What we're looking for is the motivation behind them. For example, let's look at the health insurance item. I can see how that can be motivated by a fear of someone quitting, when we approach it with the attitude, 'If you leave, you'll lose.' However, when we approach it with an attitude of love, we'll instead be thinking, 'I care about your health and don't want to see you in a health-related challenge – I wonder if there's something we can do to keep you here where your health coverage is better.' The checklist item is the same – address their current health insurance benefit – but the motivations are entirely different."

Gail had an idea. "Why don't we, as an executive team, go through and review all of our policies, assessing them to determine if what we've been doing has been motivated by fear or by love?"

"Good idea, Gail," Simon contributed. "I have a slight variation on your idea. I'd like to issue a company memo, outlining how our board meeting revealed we are often leading with fear instead of with love. All of our employees know that number one on our mission statement is to lead with love. I'd guess they've all felt times when we've led with fear, so this is not news to them. Let's ask them if any of our policies have ever made them afraid to quit. And let's listen honestly to their feedback. I'd like to take it one step further. With your permission, Gail, and with Archie's, I'd like to reach out to everyone who has quit the company in the past year, and explore this same idea with them."

"That's a huge risk, Simon," Archie was hesitant. "But I think it does reflect love. It certainly wouldn't be hurtful to our current or past employees, and I suppose that love sometimes includes the risk of making ourselves look weak or wrong. I'll green-light that."

Simon had one more idea. "Let's introduce this memo with a new tagline: 'If you don't feel loved at AMT, we want you to quit!'"

Archie didn't like that idea, but took a moment to think before he offered a reply. "I think that's the wrong message, Simon, or at least the wrong timing. I agree with the sentiment behind it, but I wonder if we would do better to focus on creating an environment of love with our actions, rather than by introducing a new slogan."

Everyone agreed with Archie on that one. As they discussed it, they realized it would be a good guiding idea for the executive team, but pushing it down to the employees was not right, at least not yet.

Chapter 6

Receiving Responses

Simon started by setting up an anonymous online survey to allow current and former employees to express themselves freely without concern of retribution. He knew that even though AMT's employees generally trusted their management, people had personal and life experiences that caused them to be guarded when criticizing, and he knew the executive team needed the unvarnished truth. Once he tested the survey, he sent out the memo:

AMT Team,

As you know, our mission statement starts with 'Lead with love'. We see this as saying two things, first that we are all leaders, and that we must lead with love; and second that when we do something, love comes first.

In our monthly board meeting we explored the idea that the AMT leadership team has some work to do in this area. We discussed how fear creeps in, often unnoticed and

*unchecked, and displaces love in our organization. We
talked about how fear and love cannot coexist.*

*We need your help. Have you felt fear at AMT? How did it
show up? When did it show up? What did it look like?
What would the situation have looked like if love showed
up in place of fear?*

*I understand that it might be tough for some of you to
express yourselves in this area; as a board it was difficult
for us to really understand it without some guidance. We
have created an online survey that will walk you through
some of the activities at AMT and solicit your perspectives.
You can follow the link at the bottom of this memo to access
it, and you can submit it anonymously or use your real
name. Also, feel free to simply reply to this email with
thoughts, or to schedule an appointment with myself or
any other member of the executive team to discuss your
feelings and ideas.*

*Rest assured we are serious about this exercise. We are
deeply committed to making AMT a company that Leads
with Love. Together, we can make this happen.*

Simon

Simon also contacted the former employees of AMT, the ones who had left within the past year, with a slightly modified version of the same message.

As soon as the first few responses arrived, Simon took them to Archie's office. He found Gail and Archie discussing what they thought the employees might say.

"Hey Simon," Archie greeted him. "Gail and I were just talking. We feel it's best to give this process one week before we dive into the responses. There are a few people who have asked for some face-time, and we want to give everyone a chance to be heard."

"Sounds good," Simon replied. "I have some responses here, but I'll hold on to them for now. Can we carve out next Wednesday afternoon to go over the responses together?"

They pulled out their phones and set a block on their calendar from Wednesday at noon until 5:30. "Let's start it with lunch," Archie offered, "and take as long as we need to look over the data."

Wednesday rolled around, and each member of the team had their notes from conversations and emails with employees. Simon had the results of the online survey, along with a chart indicating the frequency of problem areas. They met in Archie's office, where his assistant had delivered each of their favorite lunches from Mario's. They took their seats around the pub table Archie had for gatherings such as this.

Archie opened the meeting. "I was surprised at how willing people were to respond to your memo, Simon. I think people are naturally attracted to the idea of leading with love, and they are eager to point out ideas that will help us improve. I guess this is a strong confirmation of the value of the idea we adopted last year, that each person at AMT is safe to express their individuality and that every opinion is worth hearing. I think our people feel safe expressing their ideas and opinions, and I think that's a strong indication of where leading with love is working."

"I agree," offered Gail. "I was a little skeptical that we'd get much out of this. But in my meetings, people kept repeating some version of the theme that they felt safe expressing themselves. I think we were wise to listen to Tim a year ago when we had that talk about diversity of perspective and opinion, and how we need to constantly be aware of defending our position in favor of hearing someone else's. I think that's the foundation for loving relationships, and we did get that right."

Archie thought back to his own recent turning point on Valentine's Day. He remembered how, shortly after that, his friend James had called him.

"I don't get it," James sighed, "Shelly wants a divorce, but we don't really have any problems in our marriage. There has been no abuse or infidelity, and she won't tell me what's wrong."

Archie talked this over with Martha. "We've got to do something for James and Shelly. Their marriage is in trouble."

Martha called Shelly and set a date at Mug O'Joe.

Shelley was eager to pour out her heart to Martha. "Martha, you have no idea how it feels. Every time I try to open up to James, he feels like I'm attacking him. I'm really not. He's always defending himself, pointing out that he's a hard-working, kind guy and it makes me feel like there's something wrong with me. I feel like he's never actually listening to me, that every time I talk, he's only thinking about himself and how he can make sure he looks like he's got it all together. We have some problems – they're not huge, but I can't bring them up. I feel like the only outcome is that I'll feel like crap and nothing will change. I want to start over with someone else."

"I know that feeling exactly," Martha concurred. "Have you found someone else?"

"No, I haven't even looked. But I've got to imagine there are a million guys who will listen to their wives, and if one came along tomorrow, I think I'd jump on the opportunity. My heart is weary."

"I was right there," Martha empathized, "and our marriage was exactly where yours is. I couldn't talk to Archie about it, he just wouldn't listen. So I went to Tim and told him I was going to leave Archie if we couldn't resolve this."

"You were going to leave Archie?!?" Shelly was obviously surprised. "But you guys have the perfect marriage!"

"Yes, sadly, I was ready to take that step. I didn't want to. Everything in me wanted to stay and make it work. But I just didn't see how that was going to happen. I felt like every attempt ended in defeat, and I couldn't take losing any more. Like you, I thought there must be something better, and I deserved better. But Tim helped us turn it around."

"What did he do for Archie?" Shelly's curiosity was palpable. "Did he send him for counseling, or set up an accountability relationship? Was there a book he told Archie to read?"

Martha chuckled, "No, those things had already happened, and they didn't solve the problem. The way Archie explained it, Tim told him three things. Archie even wrote the three ideas in marker on our bathroom mirror. As I recall, these were his three instructions:

- *Team: Understand that your wife is on your team. She is*

not trying to attack "you", she is defending "us".

- *Communication: Understand that there is meaning and value in what your wife says. Stop focusing on her words and focus instead on understanding the meaning and emotion she is experiencing and conveying.*

- *Defensiveness: You have the right to defend yourself to your wife. Give up that right, it is the roadblock in your communication. Also realize that offering quick solutions - when not asked for - is a form of defending your value. Don't defend, listen.*

"Shelly," Martha continued, "Archie read those three ideas every day, over and over, until he'd memorized them. He also gave me the freedom to challenge him when I felt he was missing one of the three. It was that freedom that allowed me to call him out on his unloving behavior on Valentine's Day – you remember that story?"

Shelly remembered it well. She was jealous. She wished that she could've had a similar conversation with James, but she knew that such a conversation would have left him feeling self-righteous and angry, and left her feeling defeated and misunderstood.

"Could Archie share these three ideas with James?" Shelly inquired.

"He is," Martha responded, "right now at Starbucks."

After Archie's initial conversation with Tim, the one that led to writing on the bathroom mirror, he had invited Tim to share his three ideas with the executive team at AMT. Although they were slightly modified to suit the work environment, the executive team was on board with the concepts. It was this meeting that enhanced the feeling of safety at AMT – where employees felt secure in expressing their ideas and opinions to management. This was the foundation for the high quantity of honest responses they'd received from Simon's memo.

Chapter 7

Reviewing Responses

"Okay, let's take a look. I think we've got enough information to identify some patterns," Archie opened up the floor to the other two. "What most stood out to you?"

Gail went first. "There were a few things that were no surprise. These were the problems I'd already realized in the board meeting. Our people feel like we have a stranglehold on them. They want to be here, but they certainly do fear leaving."

"Can you read us some of the comments or summaries on that topic?" Archie was interested in hearing it straight from the horse's mouth.

Simon stood up and grabbed the marker. "I'll write them on the whiteboard while you read them out." He started writing Gail's words, abbreviating some longer ideas into bullet points.

- *The way you made me sign the six month letter before going for training makes me suspect I'm going to learn something in training that makes me want to leave AMT. It makes me wonder if I can trust the process.*

- *When you offered me the extended paternity leave for my first child, I was ecstatic! But then you threw in the thing about returning on the scheduled day or losing the entire block from my vacation time. That seemed a little nitpicky, and I resented it. Even though I returned on the scheduled day, this bothered me the entire time I was home with my girlfriend and baby.*

- *When I told my boss I planned to take a year off to study abroad, and wanted to know if I'd still have a job opportunity upon returning, the first thing she did was told me how I'd lose my health insurance and something bad might happen to me. It didn't seem like she cared at all about my ambitions or goals, it was really irritating.*

- *On my recent performance evaluation, it seemed like my supervisor was entirely inattentive to the issues I brought up. When he did pay attention, he doubted my honesty and contested the validity of my perspective.*

- *When I was up for a promotion, my manager suddenly got mean and spiteful. I don't know if he was afraid to lose me in his department, or jealous that I was up for promotion after seven months.*

"Can you hold there for a second?" Archie stopped Gail from

speaking and Simon from writing. "I have the picture on my phone from Simon's whiteboard – the one where we talked about what love isn't. I'd like to cross-check that list against the words our employees are using."

Archie pulled up the image he'd snapped of Simon's boardroom whiteboard, and scanned the word list. "Simon, can you write these along one side of the board?"

> *suspecting, distrusting, nitpicky, resentful, uncaring, irritating, inattentive, doubting, contesting, mean, spiteful, jealous*

"It seems that every one of these responses includes more than one of the words that describe what love isn't, from our earlier meeting," Archie commented. "This proves Tim right, but more importantly, it shows us how we are received compared to how we think we're leading. "

Archie continued, "I think this is a classic case of *intent* versus *impact*. As a leadership team, we have been evaluating ourselves by our intent – we truly do intend to lead with love. But the impact shows up differently. The impact is that our employees feel unloved. Not always, but enough that it should prompt us to reconsider our effectiveness. When the impact doesn't match the intent, we are ineffective."

"I certainly don't like it," Gail added. "This disconnect between what we mean to do and what ends up happening is unsettling. I know that in communication there are always some disconnects, but this is our number one mission, and I feel like we're falling short."

"True," Simon's turn to speak came around, "but this doesn't make us failures. The only failure is when we refuse to see it. Now that we know our impact is different from our intention, we have a target to shoot toward. Armed with this new discovery, what do we do?"

"We've come back to the starting point, but now we have a clear awareness of what we're up against," Archie was formulating a plan as he spoke. "Tim wondered about our first mission, and we now know that indeed we have work to do. Gail observed that our policies create fear, and I think we've proven that, too. Let's take a look at the responses and see if we can categorize them into the areas of the business they reflect, to turn our new understanding into action."

"Well, we've already got policies," Simon offered, and wrote it down. What else?"

The trio read and re-read the responses, eventually settling on the following list of business areas with the greatest need for improvement:

- *Policies*

- *Meetings*

- *Evaluations/Reviews*

"I'm not sure this is helpful," Simon pondered. "This is pretty much everywhere there is interaction between the leadership and the staff. We could make a very short list that says, 'Interactions'."

"You're absolutely right, Simon," Archie affirmed. "While leading with love starts in our attitudes and approaches, what we're dealing with is where the rubber hits the road. It's true that love starts in the heart, but in order for it to be received, we have to look at the interactions. The interactions are where love is felt, and if it's not there, it's actually nowhere."

This exercise was a huge step in humility for Archie, and for Simon, too. As business leaders they gained confidence in doing the right things with the right motives. This was a hard pill to swallow, that right action and right motivation didn't really amount to much if there was a chasm between it and what was felt by the recipient. Most leaders would have resorted to saying the same thing, more loudly, or more frequently, knowing they were right. But Archie and Simon had each experienced a crisis in their personal relationships that had revealed the futility of such an approach, and were willing to accept a different approach.

Gail came from a different position. She also understood the futility of saying the wrong thing more loudly, but she wasn't confident she knew the right thing to say. This new step would take a trio, and thankfully all three were fully on board.

Something had to be done if they were going to keep with their mission, and stay in business long enough to see the outcome of their approach.

Chapter 8

Penetrating Policies

"This policy issue keeps haunting me," Gail confessed. "Most of these policy problems are things I put in place to protect the company from abuse. I'm worried if we change them, we open ourselves up to all sorts of potential predicaments."

Archie agreed. "I think it would be foolish to knock down all the fences. But I have to wonder if we're building fences where they don't belong. Do we have a yard or a maze?"

"Actually," Gail said, "we have a little bit of both. I think we always start out with a yard, building the necessary fences for people to be confident that they know where they are, and where they are supposed to go. But every time someone jumps a fence, or pushes up against it, we revisit the policy and sometimes end up creating a maze."

"I can confirm that," Simon added. "I remember last month I was on a business trip. As you know, executives share the same travel reimbursement policy as everyone else in the company. I was sitting in the airport with a mild headache, and decided to pop into a shop to get some aspirin. Before I did, I figured I'd look up our expense policy to see if this was covered. Granted, I would have bought the aspirin anyhow, but I wanted to know. I wondered if some of our lower paid team members would have lived with the headache rather than shell out a few dollars of their own money. Let me tell you, that policy is a maze! There's something in there about trips where the meeting ends on one day but it's too late to get a return flight that night, and another about what you can do in the first hour after a trip ends. I actually discovered that my airport parking is not reimbursable if my luggage takes too long to come out to the carousel!"

"That's exactly what I'm talking about," Gail stated. "We started with a basic framework and then kept adding to it when someone abused the policy. Now we're fairly protected as a company, but I can imagine if someone is at the airport with a headache and the company won't buy them an aspirin, they won't feel loved. In fact, the very process of having to read through the policy brings up a lot of words on the *love isn't* list, words like irritating, exasperating, burdensome, bothersome, unhelpful, nitpicking, and mistrusting."

"Good observation, Gail," Archie responded, "and I can't help but think – maybe many of the policies we have enacted because of someone's abuse would have been better addressed in a conversation with that person. Enacting them as policy for everyone seems to add to everyone's burden, with no clear benefit."

"But I hate those conversations," Gail moaned. "They seem to always end in an argument, and our employees think it's unfair that they're subjected to something that's not in the policy."

"Let's make it part of the policy then," Simon pronounced. "But let's make it the fence around the yard, and not the maze."

"Do you have an idea?" Archie asked him.

"How about this?" Simon went to the whiteboard and wrote:

"Expenses incurred on behalf of the company are reimbursable when they are required for the company's purposes when conducting business on behalf of the company, so long as all expenses are reasonable and occur within the timeframe of the company event, including extended timeframes due to unforeseen complications."

"A step in the right direction," Archie was pleased, "that gets rid of three pages of the maze, but I think we can do better. How about this: 'When spending the company's money, realize it's for the company. You are an essential part of the company, so take care of yourself, and be reasonable. Spend the company's money as if you ran the company.'"

Simon loved the succinctness of this policy, but Gail saw a problem. "I think this leaves a lot of room for uncertainty. These people don't run this company, and don't often have to make decisions like this. I think this might be unhelpful in a different way."

"I can see where you're coming from," Archie acknowledged. "So let's add to it. What about this: 'We trust your judgment, if we didn't, we wouldn't have asked you to do the company's business. So use your best judgment. If you make a mistake, we'll talk about it, but be assured that your first mistake on any spending decision will be covered by the company and we'll call it a learning experience for both of us.'"

"I like it," Gail smiled, "but what if someone makes a huge error in judgment? What if they buy a new Ferrari on the company's dime?"

"First of all, I don't think that's going to happen," Archie clarified. "I think the people we hire are all smart people, and know – at least to some degree – what's reasonable. But if that did happen, we'd have a talk with the employee, and the company would own a new Ferrari. Then I'd give it to you, Gail, you deserve it."

"In that case, let's make sure they buy a Jaguar!" Gail laughed.

"But seriously," Archie continued, "undoubtedly everyone has different interpretations of what is reasonable. Mistakes will be made, and conversations will be had. But if I were a betting man, I would bet this will actually reduce expenses. I think our current policy unintentionally encourages people to get away with the most they can. I believe this new policy will cause people to think differently about company expenses, and spend less. I think this policy also takes out the impact of feeling unloved, and communicates trust to our people – who we know we already trust, but our policy doesn't make them feel it. Let's try it for ninety days, and keep an eye on the actual numbers. The board will obviously want the numbers, and I think they'll prove to us that when people feel loved by the company, they have a stronger tendency to act in the best interests of the company."

All three agreed. Ninety days was the right timeframe. Long enough for people to get comfortable with it, for questions to be answered, and for problems to surface. But short enough so that if they'd missed something critical, it wouldn't cause devastation. And also brief enough that if it needed to be changed back, nobody would feel like the rug had been pulled out from under them.

"Just to clarify," Simon asked, "we are still keeping the same policy for everyone at every level in the company?"

"Absolutely," Archie confirmed. "While the purchases may be different, the policy is the same. For example, as the executive team, we may be entertaining another CEO instead of an engineer, and might be buying an expensive bottle of wine over a bottle of beer with dinner. The same policy that we've written covers both. If we do have an engineer who buys a $500 bottle of Opus One, we'll have a talk with them, but we'll cover it. And we'll be happy that our engineer and his guest were able to enjoy that wine, at least once in their lives!"

They spent the rest of the afternoon reviewing and rewriting other policies. With each one, they looked for the mazes that had replaced yards, and looked for places where their impact differed from their intent. They analyzed the responses for the *love isn't* words, working them out of the equation wherever possible.

Chapter 9

Modifying Meetings

"Meetings are a tough one," Simon initiated their next session for addressing what love isn't and where fear is.

"While some of the comments pertained to how meetings were structured, most were about real-time interactions in the meetings. Things like being cut short, or hearing muffled laughter or sudden suspicous typing when an opinion was presented."

Simon had experience with this in his personal life. As a natural strategist, logic and linear thinking were part of his brain's wiring. He was a quick thinker and always had solutions. This served him well when he was sitting in front of a computer screen, but not so well when he was interacting with people.

He recalled a recent incident on a Saturday, when his wife

Francine had gone shopping. His phone rang.

"Simon," it was Francine. "I'm at the mall, and the car won't start. I've had a long day of shopping and I'm so worn out and frustrated!" She was almost crying.

Simon confirmed her location and told her he'd be right there. He hopped in his SUV and headed over to the mall.

He found her exactly where she said she'd be – of course, she couldn't go far. He greeted Francine quickly as she held the keys out to him. Stepping into the car and inserting the key, he saw the security icon flashing on the dashboard.

"Francine," Simon rolled his eyes, "do you seriously not remember the security icon? It means someone bumped into the car or something in the parking lot, and you have to press the door unlock button twice to deactivate it. Of course the car wouldn't start! Click it twice, and you're good to go."

"Thanks Simon," Francine offered meekly. "I'll see you at home."

Later that evening, Francine approached her husband. "Simon, I want to talk about today. Permission to speak freely?"

"Of course," Simon responded as he put his Kindle on the end table.

"Well, today when the car wouldn't start, I was tired and frustrated, and I obviously wasn't remembering the thing about the security icon. I hated to bother you on your day off, but I needed you."

"I'm glad it was resolved quickly," Simon thought he was finishing the conversation.

"It wasn't resolved at all," Francine continued. "I wanted the car to start, for sure. But what I needed is to have someone share in my frustration. I needed you to say something like, 'don't worry Francine, I'll be there with you in a minute,' and then when you arrived, I needed a hug, not a lecture. You solved every problem I had except the main one – to make me feel like I'm valuable to you. I felt like a nuisance to you."

Uh oh. This was a recurring theme for Simon. He was so quick to judge the situation and come up with a solution that he neglected the humanity. He lost the opportunities he had to connect with people and make them feel valued.

As he matured, Simon had learned to guard his tongue and not use mean words. But his facial expressions and the way he skipped right past understanding someone's pain left everyone feeling like they were a nuisance to him.

After reading every self-help book, it had been Tim who'd helped Simon through this one, after a request from Francine. Tim had offered Simon three ideas to memorize and build into his life.

- *Problems: A problem is an opportunity to connect with another person. The first place to connect is with their aloneness and the emotions they're experiencing. Don't even think about solving the problem until the person feels that you're with them in the problem and you've explored the emotions they're experiencing.*

- *Open Up: Fast solutions embrace data and ignore nuance, but humans are nuanced creatures. Before solving another human's problem, connect to it, and see all the opportunities that the problem holds. Be open to possibilities based on the nuance while holding the data back for a moment.*

- *Reflect: After every solution, allow time for reflection. Reflect by yourself, asking yourself if you really saw all that was behind the problem, and if your solution addressed it fully. But also reflect with the person who presented the problem, asking them if you made them feel understood and valued. Make this a priority in your schedule.*

This was no easy task for Simon. His mind raced when a problem showed up, and he was lightening-fast at coming up with solutions. But he was not an island, and although people valued him as a problem solver, they avoided deep relationships with him. It left Francine feeling isolated. Although Simon fixed things, she didn't feel the deep connection with him that she saw in other couples.

Simon was committed to adopting Tim's wisdom, but it didn't happen overnight. New situations constantly presented themselves and challenged him to slow down, connect, and reflect. He often missed it, but was grateful that Francine was the world's most patient person. Francine was just glad he was willing to grow. She didn't need perfection, she just wanted progress. And Simon was progressing.

"I don't have the perfect solution for meetings," Simon continued the conversation with Archie and Gail, "since they involve everyone. It's not something where the leadership can simply make a change and have it flow through to the organization."

"That is indeed a problem," Archie agreed. "But we can start by setting the example. As an executive team, we can all commit to making everyone feel love instead of fear at our meetings."

"I think we can go a step further," Gail advised. "I don't think anyone wants to encourage fear in a meeting. I think most of the things people are doing, they're doing because they don't understand the impact. Why don't we create some clear ground rules for meetings? We can outline them in our conference rooms, and we can exemplify them in how we conduct ourselves."

"I'm with you," Archie concurred. "Some simple ground rules. Are any of our *love isn't* words showing up in employee responses about meetings?"

Simon and Gail looked over their summaries, and Simon took to the whiteboard again to write down a list:

arrogant, rude, forceful, complaining, impatient, inconsiderate, quarrelsome, cynical, sarcastic, inattentive, crabby, cranky, snarky, dismissive, combative, evading

Simon offered a solution. "How about we make this the ground rule: 'Thou shalt not be arrogant, rude, forceful, complaining, impatient, inconsiderate, quarrelsome, cynical, sarcastic, inattentive, crabby, cranky, snarky, dismissive, combative, or evading in meetings.'?"

The others knew he was joking, but the idea was not half-bad.

Archie spoke first. "Well, that would be a good list for us to check ourselves against, after the fact. If we've made someone feel that way, we've obviously done something wrong. However, those are outcomes, not really ideas for how to conduct ourselves. I think we can dig deeper and come up with something workable."

They discussed the problems as evidenced by the survey responses, and eventually settled on three ground rules for AMT meetings:

- *The right to be heard. Everyone who is invited to speak has a right to be heard. None of us is as smart as all of us, which means that we have to be willing to give everyone a chance to say their piece, and listen. Those who are more reserved may even have to be invited to speak.*

- *The freedom to be wrong. Nobody bats a thousand, and nobody hits a home run without swinging. Everyone has the right to share an opinion without feeling shame if they're wrong. Meetings are for expression – and criticism and condemnation are sure ways to silence possibilities.*

- *The responsibility to be quiet. In order for everyone to be heard, most of us will spend the majority of each meeting being quiet. We will not step on others' conversations, and we will not be quick to respond to, or to judge, what is said.*

- *The opportunity to bring our best self. Meetings are no place for the crank, the crab, and the grouch. If you cannot be hopeful, helpful, and positive, excuse yourself from the meeting, preferably before it starts.*

Chapter 10

Repairing Reviews

"Evaluations and reviews are my domain, I suppose," Gail introduced the discussion topic of their next meeting. As the top of the food chain in HR, this buck stopped with her. "I think this is another one where our intent is right, but our impact is wrong. Our responses have more *love isn't* words in this group than any other."

"Can we list some of those *love isn't* words on the whiteboard, Simon?" Archie asked.

Simon already held the marker, and wrote down what Gail offered.

> *rejoicing at wrong, exasperating, uncaring, caustic, enraging, nagging, thoughtless, unhelpful, defeating, mistrusting, rejecting, spurning, contesting*

"That's a sad list," Archie observed. "I thought we had agreed the purpose of evaluations and reviews was to find out what people are doing right and encouraging more of the same behavior?"

"That's what we say," Gail countered, "but not what we do. In fact, most of the time when someone makes a mistake our supervisors don't address it head on, instead making a note for their next evaluation. By the time the review comes around, we have a laundry list of everything they've done wrong, and whether those things are directly addressed in the review or not, that's the backdrop that every supervisor enters the review with. It's no surprise, honestly, that people feel negative after a review, even if they get a raise."

"Can we get to the source of this approach?" Archie inquired.

Gail looked down at her feet. "It's me."

Gail was the daughter of a hard working mine foreman. Her dad worked in the dark every day, with a bunch of rough, tough men. When he came home at dinner time, he'd had enough of dealing with problems. He would grab a beer and sit in front of the TV for a couple of hours to unwind.

"Be sure not to bring up problems to your dad when he gets home," her mom would implore the children. "Wait till he's relaxed. I'll tell you when it's safe to discuss things."

The safe moments rarely came. Instead, weeks would pass with no such conversations, until one day Gail would find herself in bed, pulling the sheets over her head to insulate herself from the yelling she heard downstairs.

"You have no idea how much it hurt Gail when you missed her school play!" Her mom would yell. "And you didn't even sign her birthday card that I asked you to. I had to sign your name to it! I hate you and what you're doing to our children!"

When Gail married, she'd found a hard working man named Ted who always provided well for them. However, she found it difficult to share the day's challenges with him. He wasn't mean, it was just never the right time.

Gail would store all this up for weeks, sometimes months or years, before she'd explode. She hadn't forgotten any of the problems, she just neatly filed them all inside until they couldn't fit anymore. Their fights were rare, but ugly. So ugly, in fact, that Gail refused to have children, afraid to repeat the cycle she'd endured as a little girl and then a wife.

Ted knew Tim from Gail's work events, and called him one night after an especially bitter fight. "Tim, I don't want to leave my wife.

But she's a rageaholic. I don't know if she's got bipolar disorder or what, but I really can't live with this anymore."

Tim met with Ted a couple of days later. "Sorry for bringing you into this," Ted began, "but my wife has some serious anger problems. Can you fix this?"

Tim listened as Ted revealed the cycle of their relationship. Ted held nothing back. He wasn't eager to make Gail look bad to a work friend, but knew being secretive wouldn't give Tim the information he needed to address the issue.

After getting the full picture from her childhood to their honeymoon through to this week, Tim sat back and thought. A moment later, he leaned forward.

"Ted, you didn't start this problem, but you didn't solve it either. Gail's dad is deceased, but the problem continues, and now it's yours. Are you willing to own the problem?"

"I am," Ted was contrite and hopeful. "When I said 'I do', it was without conditions."

"It's going to take patience. Are you a patient man?" Tim inquired.

"Not really, I suppose. But I've solved this by putting the things that bother me off to the side until later. I like to push through things, so I let them accumulate until I can deal with all of them at once. But no, I'm not really patient with things as they come up."

"If that works for you, that's fine," Tim explained, "but Gail doesn't work that way. For her, and for most people, problems are like yeast. She can stuff them, but they continue to grow in a dark corner until they come out in an ugly way. This is not a symptom of bipolar disorder, this is simply the way that most people are wired. It's actually quite normal. But in order to be healthy, you can't force her to stuff her problems for a later day like you do."

"I have a three-part prescription for your relationship," Tim continued, "but this is medicine for you to take, not her. When you're strong in these three areas, you'll see a healing of the hurt Gail experienced as a girl, and still experiences in your marriage."

Tim wrote down his three ideas for Ted:

- *Observe: When Gail is experiencing something negative, it may not show up in her words, but it will show up on her face and in her body language. Be a student of this, these will be the times to approach Gail and invite her to share what's on her mind.*

- *Talk: Make it a priority to talk with Gail. Turn off the TV and put down your reading material. Give her time to talk about her day and all the good and bad it contained. Avoid being quick to offer solutions, instead, listen. Let her speak freely and listen intently. Do this every day. If either of you are out of town, schedule a time to do this by phone.*

- *Relax: Gail works hard, so do you. Make intentional time to relax together. Take a vacation. Plan weekend excursions. And realize that Gail's work doesn't end when she gets home. You guys have more money than you need. Bring in a housekeeper once a week to reduce her load, and tell her you're happy to go out for dinner on days where she doesn't feel up to preparing a meal.*

Ted took this advice to heart, and shared it with Gail. At first she found herself offended that Ted had shared intimate details with Tim. After thinking through it, she recognized Ted's desire to solve this problem in their marriage.

Initially Gail was reluctant to burden Ted with the details of her day. But Ted had become a student of her expressions, and would approach her at the right time with an invitation to share. Over time, and with Ted's consistent commitment to spending at least thirty minutes each day ready to listen, she began to open up.

Gail never exploded again.

Gail continued her explanation to Archie. "All my life I've felt like I had to save bad news for a later day, for the right time. When a supervisor would approach me to report an employee's poor behavior, I'd tell them to make a note of it for their evaluation. I've trained our team to avoid confrontation in the moment, and transferred it all to the review process."

Archie understood. "We're all a bit like that Gail," he affirmed, "that's not unusual, but it is unproductive. We need to have clean conflict in the moment, or at least before the end of the day, to make the whole cycle healthy."

Gail knew this was true. She'd experienced it for herself, in her own marriage.

Simon spoke up, "I think our stated intention for reviews is good. We find out what people are doing right and encourage more of the same behavior. I suspect the fundamental flaw of our reviews is an issue of frequency – there are issues that need to be dealt with daily, but we're making them quarterly issues. The review should be a natural outflowing of what's happening every day, and give us opportunity to course-correct and reinforce."

"We're on the same page," Archie confirmed. "Our problem is not so much in the evaluations and reviews, but in the way we address problems and deal with conflict."

"Should we come up with a conflict manifesto?" Simon was

catching on to the theme of how they were working through the employee responses.

"This one is sort of like our issue with meetings, but it's a long-term process," Archie explained. "I'm not quite sure how to go after it."

"Could Tim's advice for Ted work for anyone?" Gail wondered aloud.

Archie and Simon looked at each other. Maybe Tim had the answer, yet again.

"Let's re-work Tim's advice into something each person can do every day," Archie offered. "Simon, write this down. Let's call it 'Every Day I Will'."

- *Pay attention to my team, especially the things that bother them, as evidenced by their expressions, body language, and words.*

- *Create an opportunity for my team to express their frustrations and problems to me.*

- *Be quick and clear about expressing problems caused by my team. Address them privately and individually, avoiding a spirit of condemnation.*

- *Create an environment where my team can relax and enjoy*

their work and their work relationships.

"Wait," Simon realized, "that third point was not a part of Tim's advice."

"True," agreed Archie, "it's not. Tim's advice was based exclusively on relationship, not on production. Work relationships have another component; supervisors and managers are responsible for keeping their team on track with company goals. While a marriage may not need it in this way, the workplace needs a mechanism to address this."

This made perfect sense to Simon, and even more to Gail. In fact, she'd spent most of her married life feeling like it was just a continuation of work, and she didn't like that one bit. She had a boss at work, she certainly didn't want one at home, too. But she fully understood its place and purpose in the company.

Chapter 11

Getting Started

The trio had just started down this road of truly leading with love, and they were off to a great start. They had recognized the essential elements, and set up a healthy pattern in assessing and resolving their problem areas.

They created a template to use for future issues, one they could easily share with all levels of their team to do their own work. Here's how their template looked:

Step 1	Review the mission and values we're trying to clarify. In our case, it is Lead with Love.
Step 2	Discern the negation of our mission. What are the things we will see when we are off mission?
Step 3	Discover our present impact in the responses of those whom we are affecting.

Step 4	Determine the hidden motivations and drives that cause negative expressions or responses to show up.

Step 5	Address issues causing a negative impact by re-focusing on our mission while understanding our motivations.

Step 6	Measure results – always by impact, never by intention.

After revising policies and setting some new standards for meetings and reviews (which was actually a standard for all interactions), Simon set up a number of town-hall style meetings to discuss these changes with everyone at AMT. He clearly articulated the reasoning of the executive team, and how he hoped these changes would give them a clearer course toward their mission. He invited feedback from everyone in the company, assuring them the executive team was no longer measuring their success by their intent, but by their impact to each and every team member.

After ninety days, Simon sent out another memo. He had refined the survey slightly, and summoned new responses to their three areas of focus. The results were positive – while there was still work to do, the fear was diminishing and the *love isn't* words weren't nearly as prevalent.

In the meantime, Gail received a phone call.

"Hi Gail, it's Damian Lloyd."

Damian had been a rising star at AMT. One of their top engineers, he had been through advanced training with the company and was on track to be the Director of Innovation. But suddenly, and without much explanation, he left the company.

"Hey Damian! Good to hear from you," Gail really liked Damian. He was one of her favorites. "How is your new deal going?"

"I don't have a new deal. I need to level with you – I left AMT because I felt strangled and controlled. I enjoyed the environment, but it felt kinda like a minimum security prison. Everyone was nice to the inmates, you were especially nice, but it wasn't the place I wanted to be. I still keep in touch with a lot of the engineers at AMT, and they say that feeling is gone. They tell me it's like a new company. I'm calling to ask – would you consider hiring me back?"

This was not the only such call Gail would receive in the coming months. At AMT, their impact was finally coming in line with their intent, and it was good.

Part 2

The Story of You as a Leader

Chapter 12

Must We Lead with Love?

In any organization, one of the most important things is to be true to your mission. The mission doesn't have to be 'Lead with Love', but as we evolve as a species, this certainly isn't a bad mission to hold. In times past, there was a value to missions like 'Get more food', or 'Save the children from the Spinosaurus'. However, in this era, and in developed nations, we should be beyond those.

We've seen many companies in our era who lead with love. Their performance, retention, and balance sheets seem to eclipse other companies in their marketplace. If this isn't a part of your company's values, it's worth consideration.

There are two organizations in which the mission to lead with love is not an option – it's a mandate. These are the family and the church.

Don't get me wrong, very few people go into a marriage without this mission. And even fewer have children without committing to love them, with notable exceptions like Genghis Khan, perhaps. And although some religious organizations have been started for selfish gain, most start out of a motivation to love. For these, the problem is not with their intent, but with their impact.

Here is the true measure of our success in leading with love: do the people I'm leading feel loved?

I hope it's not true, but I have to wonder if we surveyed churches and families, if their responses wouldn't sound like, "I *know* I'm loved, but I'm not sure I *feel* loved." This is the sign of a leader who has a gap between their motivations and the results. This is the gap that AMT solved with their template.

If you truly have the desire to lead with love, it's time to get rid of your title and everything you do right, and get into the pasture.

Chapter 13

Into the Pasture

W hat does it mean to get into the pasture? The concept
comes from the idea of a shepherd. Jesus, the greatest
leader in recorded history (as measured by the number
and impact of his followers) didn't call himself a rabbi
(teacher/professor), a revolutionary (political leader), or a ruler
(executive), he called himself a good shepherd.

"I am the good shepherd. The good shepherd lays down his life
for the sheep...I am the good shepherd; I know my sheep and my
sheep know me...and I lay down my life for the sheep." John
10:11-15

In his description, Jesus doesn't talk about how a good shepherd
corrals sheep, or controls sheep. He talks about how much he
values sheep, so much so that he gives up his own life for them –
the greatest sacrifice that anyone can make.

I often talk with husbands who indicate the level of sacrifice they'd endure for their wives:

"I would take a bullet for my wife. I'd die for her," says husband.

"Would you turn off the TV for her, every night for a month?" ask I.

"Come on, seriously? That's an awful lot to ask," laments husband.

The truth of it is most of us, me included, live and die first for ourselves. We hold up as heroes those like Mahatma Gandhi, who refused to eat because he loved his people so deeply, or Mother Teresa, who refused to accept a Nobel Prize because of her love for her people. But these should not be exceptional heroes, these should be all of us. Mohandas and Agnes understood life in the pasture.

The reality is that very few of us are ever actually required to die for our sheep. Gandhi lived to 78 years old, Mother Teresa to 87. They lived long, full days, and death did not receive them early. Their life wasn't characterized by dying for their people, but by a *willingness* to die for their people.

Of course, there are exceptions to this – heroes who died early for their people, some unwillingly, some willingly. The common thread is that their leadership in death was at least as powerful in expanding love as any leadership in life could have been. The bottom line is that if you're truly going to lead with love, there are no limits.

Love with limits says things like, "I will do this, if you do that..." Interestingly, according to our assessment earlier in this book, that's not love at all. Call it kindness or courtesy or generosity, or whatever, but it falls short of love.

If we are truly going to lead with love, it makes sense to go through a process like Archie, Simon, and Gail did, at Tim's prompting. That process begins with a step that we alluded to, but was mostly assumed – true humility.

Chapter 14

Step 0 - Humility

Why do we call this step zero? It's the prerequisite before any worthwhile change happens. You can't start on step one without first having humility, or you'll arrive at the end of your journey still as far from your goal as when you started.

As I see it, there are two essential components of humility – how you see yourself, and how you see others.

In *A Thirty Year Journey Back to First Grade*, I described how I could fake humility with the best of them – I learned it in Seminaryland. I consistently acted humbly, but I had no humility. I saw myself as having the right answers, and I saw others as saviors or those needing saving. This was arrogance in its finest form, and I had some serious work to do before I started down the road to humility.

My first stop was in how I saw myself. I saw myself as having less worth and value than I actually had, and I believed I needed to shore that up and create value for myself by being smart and right. I wonder if any time we see someone who insists on always being right, whether it's a president or a peasant, we have to wonder if they don't see themselves with the value they truly have.

For me, I had to embrace the idea that whether I was wrong or right, whether I was smart or dumb, I was still me, and me was still worthwhile. Much like a willingness to die as exemplified in the good shepherd, I didn't need to be wrong or dumb, I just had to be willing to, and not let it reduce me to nothingness. God showed us this level of character when he fought with Jacob, or argued with Abraham. Jesus showed it when the Canaanite woman pled for the healing of her daughter. As I see it, the outcome of these situations was an odd, almost unsettling, humility. In my paraphrase, these encounters ended with, "You know, you have a good point. I've changed my mind." This didn't in any way diminish the value of God or Jesus. True humility doesn't rest on being smart or right or pretty or rich or skillful; it recognizes that those things do not define us.

The first has to take place before the second stands a chance. In the second part of humility, we have to see the intrinsic value of others. In terms of value, nobody is above us or beneath us. We are all interconnected beings in the same world on largely the same mission. Some go further faster, but we all entered the world naked and penniless; there are no exceptions. And we all end up naked and penniless. No exceptions. This means the world is not divided into the rich and the poor, the lost and the found, the pretty and the ugly, the sick and the well. Those are just the present point-in-time position of others, and in no way describe their overall position nor their value.

Jesus demonstrated this well by his choice of cohorts. He saw the value in those whom society had cast out. He didn't call them 'projects', but 'friends'. When it came time to select his board of directors, he didn't look at attractiveness or status or wealth or accomplishment; he didn't see those people as any more valuable than the fishermen he selected. In fact, when those folks used their power to point to their worth, Jesus pointed back.

Archie and Simon had learned humility at home before they could bring it to the workplace. Oftentimes that's the way it works. Nobody can reveal us to us with as much clarity as those we live with. Sadly, we can be our own worst enemy in this. In an effort to preserve the false value we've set up, we tend to reject anyone who points out that it's not real. If, like the naked emperor, we demand to be seen as valuable, we will often ignore the perspectives of our spouses and children and instead embrace the perspectives of those who butter our bread. So long as we listen to those who applaud the sizzle over the steak, we will keep sizzling until we sizzle out, leaving very little behind but a dirty pan.

There's a word for this desire to have the false value preserved at the expense of our true value; it's called defensiveness. Those who understand their intrinsic worth don't see much purpose in defending themselves. Instead, they welcome input that reveals them to themselves. And they focus on defending others. The truth is we've got a limited supply of defending energy. If we're using it on ourselves, there's not much left over for others. Do you know what you call a person who doesn't defend those he loves? You sure don't call him a leader.

We must get to the place where we recognize our immutable, intrinsic value, and see the same in others. We must give up the need to defend ourselves, instead defending others. We must listen openly and honestly to those who reveal us to us, especially at home. They are our greatest allies in the quest to lead with love.

Chapter 15

Step 1 - Mission

A re you on a mission? If not, there is little benefit to doing any work. As a human, you were designed to engage in a mission. It can morph and change over time, but realize if it's absent, so is your fulfillment. The human species was designed to go places and do things toward a mission. It's what drives us.

I anchored this book on the mission of leading with love. I think that's a noble mission for anyone who finds themselves leading a company, church, family, or any other organization. This was the mission our characters chose for themselves – at work and at home.

If you don't know your mission, stop. Take a minute to find it and clarify it. For the sake of the world, please try to find a noble mission. 'Be a good father' is another noble mission. So is 'reduce fatal car accidents'. As are 'free India from tyranny' and 'be a light to those most in need'. After many years of defining and refining my personal mission, I boiled it down to two words: 'Expand Love'.

Determining your mission is a 'you' effort, but you can certainly invite others to see into you and observe where you have uniqueness that must come out to the world. Look inside for the things that bother or relieve you. Look for your own life experiences and talents. Was your brother wrongfully convicted of a crime? Maybe your mission is to have his case re-tried, or maybe it's your mission to create awareness of the flaws in our legal system. Did you grow up on a family farm? Maybe it's your mission to shine a light on the brutality of factory farming.

Nobody can prescribe the 'right' mission for you, but for you, there is always a right mission. Maybe even a bunch of right missions.

My daughter was never a slave. But on a trip to Southeast Asia, she saw the plight of young girls who had been sold into slavery, primarily sexual slavery. She discovered her mission. It was not to free girls from slavery, although she has many friends who have that as their mission. Instead, her mission was to figure out why families sell their children as slaves in the first place. Today she lives in Phnom Penh. She brings solar light into houses, so that young girls can finish school. She equips women with computers and sewing machines so that they can engage in productive fruitful labor while raising their children. And she drills clean water wells to save families from the brutal tyranny of long walks for polluted water – with the realization that a sick sibling and work/study time reduced by the collection of water are some of the primary precursors to a child sold into sexual slavery.

74

Was it wrong for her not to adopt the mission to free enslaved girls? Not at all. This was someone else's mission, and she was not well suited for the heart-rending danger of this mission. She adopted a mission that was equally as noble, and was more 'her': discover why girls are sold, and stop it before it happens.

That is to say, there is no wrong mission for you or your company. It is what it is. But if you want to make a positive difference, find a noble mission, and one that moves you passionately.

Once you have your mission, make it clear. My mission, expand love, does not seem terribly clear. But it's the result of a ton of smaller missions, merged and distilled into one macro mission. I am aware of all the ideas that went into this two-word mission, so for me it is clear. However, if I'd jumped straight to expand love as my mission, it might lack the clarity needed to translate it into action. Your mission must make sense to you – you must know how it shows up in the world.

It's okay to start with something, and let it change over time. This is natural, and a sign of maturity. As you move in your mission, it will become more broad and more narrow at the same time. And you may even fully accomplish it, moving on to your next mission.

The bottom line is this: have a mission.

Chapter 16

Step 2 - Discerning

It's necessary to know what your mission looks like; what your world looks like when you're 'on mission'.

In AMT's case, it was helpful to understand the negation of their mission. What did it look like when they were 'off mission'? Sometimes we see the mountain most clearly from the top looking down, and other times from the bottom looking up. In reality, the clearest picture of the mountain comes when we look at it from all angles.

For my mission (expand love) and any mission centered on love, I found it extremely helpful when my guide prompted me to explore what love isn't, based on I Corinthians 13, the Bible's famous 'love chapter'. If your mission is to shine a light on the brutality of factory farming, you'll see the negation of that if you go home at Thanksgiving and discover your nephew is in the dark about how livestock are treated at these farms.

We need to be keenly aware of the difference between a negative perspective and the perspective of negation. A negative perspective often means that we expect the negative outcome to happen. In contrast, the perspective of negation allows us to discern the negative if it does happen. The latter is beneficial to our mission, the former is not.

The clearer your mission, the easier it will be to discover when you're off mission. If you're having trouble with this step, it may be time to revisit your mission and clarify it. Invite others to offer their perspectives – after all, none of us is as smart as all of us.

It's beneficial to also discern what your world looks like when you're on mission. This is the perspective from the top of the mountain looking down. When you realize what things look like from the top, you'll be inspired to throw yourself more fully into your noble mission. Read stories of people who had a similar mission, and look at their results. Be inspired by them, in fact, let their wind carry you. Know that if they did it, you can do it too, and your world will improve in the same way theirs did.

An essential part of discerning is recording. When you discern something, either through negation or otherwise, write it down. You'll need it as you move through the next steps. Don't trust this to your memory; you'll just make it hard on yourself and reduce your chance of success.

Chapter 17

Step 3 - Understanding

T rue understanding cannot be achieved in a vacuum. Isolated, all you can know is your intention, and frankly, your intentions don't really matter.

That's not to say that intentions are unimportant. They are critically important, as they give you a starting line. You can't enter the race without first finding the starting line. But when you mistake the starting line for any real accomplishment, or even for the finish line, you haven't run much of a race.

Don't give your intentions any more credit than is due them. They are merely a starting point, the beginning of a journey.

True understanding is only measured in the impact. Do you want to provide solar lighting in underdeveloped countries so girls can stay in school? Great intention. How many houses now have lights, and how many girls are staying in school? That's your impact.

We have a natural desire to measure ourselves by our intentions. This is what Archie did when he bought the velvet and crystal box of chocolates. His intentions were pure, noble, and loving. The shopkeeper and his friend James lauded him, which caused him to feel even better about himself with these wonderful intentions. But his impact was the only accurate measure. Martha received the chocolates, and did not feel loved.

This is where humility comes in. In our natural desire to protect and affirm our value by defending our intentions, we can find it difficult to hear an honest assessment of our impact. Archie knew this when his wife told him the chocolates did not make her feel loved, just as Simon knew it when Francine told him getting the car started didn't meet her deeper needs. Both men had chosen not to get their value from their rightness or their performance, but rather, to measure their impact based on the perceptions of the recipients. This is what prompted AMT's survey. They could never have understood where they fell short if they did not query their employees, and the employees never would have responded if they felt that their executives had insufficient humility to hear their perspectives – and do something about it.

I am astounded by the length of time I spent defending my false value, and I am astounded at the great lengths people will go to in defending that which doesn't matter – at the expense of that which does. I think this is what Paul is talking about prior to the love chapter, when he says, "Knowledge puffs up, but love builds up." Defending the knowledge of our intentions indeed puffs us up, making us feel bigger and better. But there is no construction in that. It is simply wasted effort that keeps us from doing the things that have a beneficial impact.

Tim expressed wisdom when he advised Archie to see his defensiveness as the roadblock to communication with his wife. As long as Archie defended himself, he would be puffed up and his relationship would not be constructed. There are times where it's beneficial to defend oneself, but they're so rare they're not even worth mentioning.

James' wife, Shelly, knew the pain of trying to have open communication with a husband who always defended his intentions. Every conversation left her feeling defeated and inferior. Eventually, she decided to stop trying, and to start over with someone else. There is a big risk in pointing out the gap between someone's intent and their impact. If the person is not humble, but is instead defensive, they will feel attacked and will retaliate. We often train our spouses, children, and coworkers to lie to us, or not talk to us at all. Nobody enjoys living in pain, especially the kind of pain that doesn't result in any improvement. There's a huge difference between the pain of a car accident and the pain of exercise. Similarly, there's a huge difference between the idea of pointing out the intent-impact gap to a defensive person and to a humble one.

At AMT, they had embarked on the process of creating a safe environment to share the shortcomings of leadership, and had done this a full year before they solicited feedback in the survey. Had they not consistently evidenced humility in having their flaws exposed, it is doubtful the survey would have accomplished much of anything.

Once we come to the realization that we need to gain understanding by assessing impact, we can expect it will be some time before those who love us are willing to be open with us. Tim challenged Ted on his patience, and indeed, patience is required when we are learning humility. It is during this phase that we shouldn't even attempt to be defensive – those that love us are testing the waters to know if they are truly safe. If an employee emails you with the message, "You're just like Hitler!" you have every right to defend yourself. But if you're ever going to understand your impact, you must give up that right. If you value that employee and want the benefit of their perspective, work to understand how you might have impacted them in a way that led to the email. An appropriate email reply might be, "I have certainly been dictatorial, mean, and uncaring, and the way I shut you down at our last meeting is clear evidence of that. I need to apologize to everyone who was at the meeting. Do you think we could have lunch? I value your input, and have been ignoring it for too long."

This may seem weak to those who are accustomed to leading with power. It is not the way of the boardroom, but it is the way of the pasture. You'll never know your sheep, so to speak, if you can't hear the impact you've had on them. And you'll never hear the impact when you're focused on your intentions, or your power or position. The way of humility is actually strength in action, and is the only way to truly know and be known. It is the way of understanding.

Chapter 18

Step 4 - Awareness

A wareness takes understanding a step deeper. Awareness requires that we know our own hidden motivations and drives.

Jonathan Haidt presents the model of the rider and the elephant. If you haven't read his books, order them now, so they'll arrive by the time you're done with this one. The way I see it, the person who has understanding knows who they are, and how what they do affects others. They know where they want to go and where others are going. But with the next step, awareness, this person knows he is actually riding an elephant, and going where the elephant takes him.

We're going to refer to the elephant a few more times. It's essential to understand the elephant is us – just like the rider is us – but we may not recognize the elephant until it's pointed out. When we decide to lose weight but grab one more slice of pizza, that's the elephant. We can know we're more likely to die from a falling coconut than a shark attack, but when we calmly walk under the coconut palms to the beach and are afraid to go in the water because that's where sharks live, that's our elephant.

The elephant encompasses the automatic processes that dominate our thinking and actions. The unaware person thinks that they are thinking. The aware person sees the thinking that's done by their elephant. Why does this matter? I wonder if it's because we trained our elephant when we were children, when we had little understanding. As we age, we risk being taken where the elephant goes – based on its immature training.

This was evidenced in the life of Gail. Growing up with a father who didn't want to hear about problems until he was ready (and he never was), Gail trained her elephant. She told her elephant not to talk about problems openly – that it was unsafe (even dangerous) to express one's own needs at a time that didn't suit the listener. When Gail's elephant went on a quest to find her a mate, it trudged through the forest to discover a safe place. Gail's elephant brought her to Ted, who was non-expressive and permitted Gail to act likewise. However, as Ted realized from Gail's rage episodes, not expressing something does not mean you don't experience something. Gail had trained her elephant while she was hiding under the covers as a young girl, and her elephant kept following its own tracks in circles, taking Gail where she did not want to go.

Why is it so hard to move into awareness? In short, because our inner voice is the loudest voice we hear. If we think we're vocal about defending ourselves to others, we should hear how we defend ourselves to us!

This is amplified in a society where certainty leads to power and power leads to security. In Tibet, the leader wears a dress and rides an exercise bicycle. He doesn't know anything for sure, except love for his people. Here in the United States, our leader wears a cadre of Secret Service guards and rides a reinforced jet with missiles. He knows everything for sure, except whether to love his people. East and West have two very different paths, but according to a Harris Interactive poll, the Dalai Lama and the President of the United States were regarded equally popular as leaders.

So when we talk to ourselves and say, "you must be right, of that you are certain," we short-circuit the path to awareness. We tell ourselves that we are protecting ourselves from ourselves, while our elephant crashes us into tree after tree.

Simon was wise to ask, "what would happen if...?" This caused the executive team at AMT to dig deeper and discover that their elephant was deathly afraid of losing people. Only after seeing this did the team have the awareness to approach the problem with the right motivations. If they'd skipped that step, their elephant never would have allowed them to make any change that threatened it.

The journey to awareness requires that we silence the internal voice that defends us. This is much harder than silencing the external voice – for that we only have to zip our lip. The internal voice keeps talking after our lips are sealed. It is ever-present, and it seems the harder we work to silence it, the louder it becomes. Take a moment now to not think about Abraham Lincoln. Did you think about Honest Abe? Hard to silence that voice, isn't it?

The folks at AMT were well served with the wisdom of their peers. When prompted, these peers asked them to look at things another way, and they gave up the certainty of being right to do so. However, what wasn't indicated is how loud the voices in their heads were, telling them, "you already have the answer!" Without an ability to silence that voice, the voice of wisdom would have been drowned out.

So what's the key to silencing that voice? Bad news here – I don't know. The best I've been able to accomplish is to quiet the voice long enough to hear the other voices. The internal voice keeps popping up, 'defending' and 'protecting' me from wisdom. After much practice, I've discovered how to discern the sound of that voice, and gently quiet it down.

King David, in his unprecedented book of poetry simply known as The Psalms, knew both voices. The person who guides his elephant, as I see King David saying, is the one who meditates on God day and night. In fact, David meditates (haghah) over and over. Haghah is a Hebrew onomatopoeic word, implying that the same sound is muttered in constant repetition, from the soul and not from the mind. Today, we would call this chanting, or mantra meditation. It's interesting that 3,000 years later, deeply spiritual people often meditate with the Sanskrit mantra, "Om Shanti, Om Shanti, Om Shanti". I've heard it said that David repeated in his Hebrew, "Shal Om, Shal Om, Shal Om." Translated to English, both are the same word – peace.

As we discover awareness, we have to be prepared for the idea that our driving motivations are neither intelligent nor mature. This should come as no surprise, as most of us trained our elephants at a very young age. We should be cautious about judging and condemning ourselves. Just like for Gail, Archie, Simon, and James, the beginning of awareness is not arriving at a destination, but truly discovering our present position. The power of awareness is that it reveals where we actually are, like placing a dot on the map, the starting point from which we can get to our destination. If all we have is the map, but no accurate awareness as to our current position, where do we go next? If we are like most people, our elephant will continue retracing its footsteps, always moving but never going anywhere.

Give it a shot: "Shal Om, Shal Om, Shal Om..." The truth may be bigger than you have ever seen.

Chapter 19

Step 5 - Focus

O kay, we have a clear map in hand, and we've plotted our current position. Now it's time for action. We need to move forward. Which way is forward, again?

As a pilot, I often have to create and file a flight plan. Sounds simple, doesn't it? Find my origin and my destination, and draw a line between. If I had a rocket ship, it would be that simple. But, alas, I do not. I'm stuck with a single engine airplane.

If my journey takes me to the next airport over, I have an uncomplicated plan. But my mission is to expand love, and that's not the next airport over. That's a long journey. So my flight plan requires focus.

Just like the trio at AMT, I have to take all of the variables and consider them in my plan. How much fuel can I carry with my projected weight of passengers and cargo? Do my planned refueling airports offer fuel service at the time I anticipate arriving? Where is the weather going and what's it doing? What are the current and projected winds aloft? Are there temporary flight restrictions or special airspaces en route? Is there terrain at my intended altitude? Where are my alternate airports? What are their runways lengths and density altitudes at the time I'll be passing over them? What about the pilot reports from others traveling my route ahead of me?

But stay focused, the two key points are where I am and where I'm going. The rest are variables, and need to be considered for the journey. There is room for these to be adapted to en route. In fact, in the next section we'll examine the importance of this.

Gail considered one variable when Simon and Archie proposed a reworking of their reimbursement policy. Remember when she said, "I think this leaves a lot of room for uncertainty."? She considered the possibilities along the route, and saw how this one could throw a wrench in their plans.

We can acquire these possibilities from two sources: first, from our own slow thinking, evaluating things within the context of our awareness and experience; and second, from the awareness and experience of others. Again, humility shows up. To truly receive the benefit of another's awareness and experience, we must approach them humbly, eager to learn. This is by far the shortest path to our destination – remember that none of us is as smart as all of us. Discernment is necessary, as everyone may not understand your destination in the way you do, or may be eager to offer advice to prove their own worth to you, without really having had the experience.

I recall one time a friend and I were hopelessly lost in Mexico City – a city three times the size of Los Angeles and not nearly as organized. We had a map, but it was a highway map, not a street map. If only we could get to a highway, we could find our way to our next destination. But we had to get out of the city.

We stopped frequently, asking those with rolled-down windows and others walking on the street to help us get out of town. Everyone we stopped was eager and willing to give us directions out of town. But eight hours later, it was getting dark and we were getting weary of finding ourselves back where we started.

Finally we happened upon a man who was willing to draw us a map. His map actually fit with our highway map, so we had confidence he was leading us accurately.

"We've been driving in circles all day," I told him, "and asking for directions frequently. All of the directions were wrong. Do you have any idea why so many people would lead us on a wild goose chase?"

"Oh, that's simple," he replied, "Mexicans are a helpful people. They'll always give directions when asked. However, most *Chilangos* have never been out of the city. You're no better off asking them how to get out of the city than you are asking that lamppost!"

So ultimately, two things were true: it was the advice of a *Chilango* that got us where we wanted to go, and it was the advice of *Chilangos* that kept us stuck. Oh, sweet discernment.

Focused on his helpful directions, and our highway map, we eventually made it to our destination.

Remember Simon? His advice from Tim helped him do a better job of finding his own solutions. There were three ideas. First, he had to gain a new perspective on problems and how people relate to them. Second, he had to open up to possibilities and truly connect. Third, he had to reflect. These three approaches helped him see problems more accurately, and focus appropriately on their resolutions.

With a focus on where you are, where you're going, and what's along the way, you can move toward your destination. But don't move too quickly; that's where measuring comes in.

Chapter 20

Step 6 - Measure

The work of flight planning doesn't stop when I barrel down the runway. That's when it starts.

Once airborne, it's time to start measuring results – remember, never by intent, always by impact.

Imagine that I am flying from San Francisco to Portland with a forecast five knot wind from the south, but the actual wind is forty knots from the west. My compass reads 'N' and my heading indicator shows '0'. I'm going north, right? Not at all. I'd be running out of fuel while I wondered who stole Portland as Spokane came into sight. In aviation, this is referred to as a difference between your 'heading' and your 'track'. I'm heading the right direction, but I'm way off track. No Voodoo Donuts for me today.

The funny thing is that with only myself and my airplane as a reference point, there is absolutely no way on earth to know I'm off track. Unless the controller below me or the satellites above me report my position, I have no idea where I am. I clearly know where I started and where I intend to go, but I have no way to know that I'm on track.

Imagine this happened, and the air traffic controller called me on the radio to tell me of my error:

Controller: "Uh, Saratoga two-two-two, state your intended destination."

Me: "I'm headed to kilo-papa-delta-xray, Portland International."

Controller: "Saratoga two-two-two, are you aware you're presently on track for Spokane?"

Me: "Excuse me sir, are you a pilot?"

Controller: "Saratoga two-two-two, negative, I'm a controller."

Me: "And sir, are you in this aircraft with me?"

Controller: "Saratoga, negative, I'm at Seattle Center."

Me: "Then sir, I kindly ask you to stop giving me advice. You have no idea what's it like up here. Flying a plane is hard work."

Controller: "Saratoga, I'm just trying to help. I have you on radar, and I can see your position more clearly than you possibly could."

Me: "Sir, you're making me angry, I didn't ask for your advice, and I don't need it."

Of course, in aviation, that conversation precedes a flight directly to the scene of my own crash, and posthumous fame on YouTube.

How stupid can a man be? Well, let's examine a similar conversation between a man, who we'll call man, and his wife, who we'll call wife:

Wife: "Is it your intention to always show our daughter love and fill her with confidence, and to be loved and appreciated by her?"

Man: "Yes, that is indeed my intention."

Wife: "Are you aware that if you miss her awards ceremony again this year, she'll be devastated, and may even grow to resent you?"

Man: "Do you have any idea what my life is like? I have to work 80 hours each week just to pay for this house and your spending habits."

Wife: "No, I don't really know what your work life is like, and the pressure that must be on you. What I do know is how our daughter responds when you miss her awards ceremonies."

Man: "Then you're in no position to judge me and tell me how I should prioritize my time."

Wife: "I'm just trying to help. I didn't know if you saw how deeply this affected her."

Man: "You're making me angry. I didn't ask for your advice, and I don't need it."

How stupid can a man be? Sadly, I am that stupid, when I measure my position by my intent and not my impact, and when I refuse to accept the advice of the allies best suited to report my position to me. Archie was this stupid, until Tim wisely advised, "Your wife is not trying to attack 'you', she is defending 'us'."

The executive team at AMT didn't implement any change without first recognizing the only group who could tell them if they were on track: their employees. They intentionally reached out to them after ninety days to get an 'impact report'. They didn't trust their own assessment of their position, they knew who could accurately report their position from the ground, and that's who they listened to.

You can do everything else right, but if you don't return to measure the results – by their impact – and correct your course, you will end up off track.

Again, Tim revealed his wisdom when he told Simon to check in with Francine every single day, even if one of them was out of town.

Frequent measurements and corrections are an absolute imperative of reaching your destination.

Part 3

When You're Wandering in the Pasture

Chapter 21

When the Mission is Misplaced

We've all seen it, the mission gets misplaced. At AMT, this almost happened when the board focused on the numbers. This could have derailed the company from their mission, had it not been for the wisdom of Tim, and the executive team's commitment and conviction.

Changing priorities, unforeseen circumstances, discouragement, and defeat all enter the journey, and all threaten to obscure the mission. Sometimes the mission gets lost in the clouds and the pressing matters of the day take over. The vice of placing the urgent before the important leaves no time to check the mission status.

This happens frequently in businesses, large and small. But more disconcerting is the frequency with which it happens in marriage and at church.

I once attended a church founded on the idea of serving the poor.

By the time I arrived many years later, this service to the poor had been reduced to a once-monthly special benevolent offering, where all of the proceeds went to the community's hungry. One Sunday, after an especially long-winded sermon, it was time for the month's benevolent offering.

"I went a little long today," the pastor apologized, "and I know how you all feel when you end up and the back of the line at Ponderosa. So we'll just dismiss now and skip the special offering."

From serving the poor to ensuring the parishioners got front-of-line position at the steakhouse – this church had lost its mission. Sadly, this is not unusual.

The mission is lost at least as often in marriage. I've wondered about making a recording that I'd sell on iTunes to women who'd been married twenty five years. It would save them from having to address their husband directly when they gave him the news. It would go something like this:

"Honey, we started off so much in love. I remember how we were going to conquer the world together and grow old in each other's arms. But then we both went to work, and kids came along, and we raised them well. But somewhere in these twenty five years, we seem to have lost our first love. There's nothing more between us. There's no future for our marriage. The kids are off at college, and I'm going to Italy with Valentino. I truly wish you the best."

Of course, I would never actually create such a recording, but I shudder to think that it might actually become a top-seller. We are misplacing our mission.

I think part of the problem is shifting baselines. Imagine if, on my flight to Portland, I found myself off track and said, "Well, I guess I'll just go to Spokane, I'm almost there anyhow." And then when I refueled in Spokane with a next planned destination of Vancouver, I said, "Vancouver seems so far away, I think I'll just go to Missoula."

In the twenty five year marriage above, it looks similar. It starts with a mission to conquer the world together. But then it's time to buy the first house, and that requires a renewed focus on the career path. Then kids come along, and that requires a bigger house, and more hours at the office. College expenses are sure to come, so the dedicated husband takes a promotion that requires a lot of time out of town, and sometimes they only talk on weekends. After twenty five years, the whole thing is so far off course that it seems easier just to start over, accompanying Valentino to Milan, or Crystal to Reno. But Valentino and Crystal are not the beautiful endings that could, and should, have been.

Churches seem caught in the same cycle. It starts with a desire to give the neighbors a spiritual home. A building is bought, and it saddles the members with debt. More members means more offerings, and a marketing campaign is launched. More people would come if the music was better, so big screens are bought and a band is hired. Somewhere along the line, the preacher yells at the video guy, who happens to live next door, for making him look bad on the videocast. The video guy leaves, saying, "I wish there was a spiritual home in my neighborhood."

The mission gets misplaced.

Ephesus is a town in Turkey. Most likely, it was the base of early Christian missionaries. The spread of Christianity has Ephesus to thank. But less than thirty years later, an angel visited a guy named John in a dream and said, "Tell the people at Ephesus that God has seen they've forgotten their first love."

The angel offered a solution:

1. *Recognize how far you've fallen.*
2. *Turn around.*
3. *Do the things you did at first.*

Smart angel. Three simple steps: recognize, repent, return. I don't think I could have said it any better.

It's never too late to get back to the pasture, and back to your mission.

Chapter 22

When Fear Pops Up

Thank God for fear. It's what caused us to turn around and look when the Spinosaurus was coming to eat our children.

Without fear, we'd be visiting *Planet of the Spinosaurus* by spacecraft.

Here's the problem with fear: it's what drove us, when as children living in a strange, confusing, dangerous world, we trained our elephants.

I lived with a constant fear. I feared that I wouldn't matter. This fear drove me to accumulate a multi-million dollar net worth by my early thirties. And this fear caused me to lose it all.

That's the odd thing about fear – it's irrational. It seems to show up most often in the places it doesn't belong.

AMT identified their fear. They were afraid of losing people. And their response to this fear actually caused them to lose important, valuable people like Damian. That's the bitter irony of fear, it often creates the very outcomes that it seeks to prevent.

Since most readers of this book were once children, I think it's fair to say that most of our fears were developed in this impressionable season of our lives – in childhood. In this season, even a cow in the shadows could resemble a Spinosaurus. Thirty years later, when our elephant encounters a cow, it retreats.

Unchecked, we'll go through life running from cows.

This often shows up in relationships. A little boy once told his mom he flunked his math test, something she didn't want to hear. The boy was banished to his room, and he felt isolated and alone. As an adult, he is fired from his job, and he knows his wife certainly won't want to hear that. So he lies to her. He senses that if he tells her the truth, he'll feel isolated again, maybe even end up alone. This doesn't make logical sense – the boy's mom didn't stop being his mom when he went to his room. She certainly didn't stop loving him. And his wife really deserves to know that he lost his job, it's a part of her life, too. But the elephant isn't driven by logic. The elephant moves in the illogical world of feelings. His elephant (which is fully him) has just broken trust with his most important ally, the one who wants to walk with him through the pain of his rejection. He has now created aloneness and isolation for himself, in the very act of trying to avoid it.

There is an antidote to fear: it's just a cow.

Like the team at AMT, our first order of business is to examine ourselves when fear pops up. Sometimes that's hard, fear can mask itself with the most clever of disguises. However, with the awareness exercise we discussed previously, and others covered elsewhere, we can check-in with ourselves and focus on our motivations. When we have a gap between intent and impact, that's an especially important place to go digging for fear. When we find it, it's important to shine the light of adult truth on it: it's just a cow, and cows don't eat people.

Sadly, most people never get to the place where they expose the fear in their motivations. It's scary. Why would we want to experience fear if we don't like the feeling of fear? I can think of many good reasons, but the first one should be enough. There are a lot of cows in the world. If we don't expose the fear now, we're going to keep experiencing it – over and over. If we don't like the feeling of fear, why would we subject ourselves to it repeatedly?

Earlier, Tim made a strong statement, "Perfect love casts out fear." This is always true, except when we chose to hold on to the fear. Love doesn't force anything, it sits by always on the ready to bring light and goodness – but it doesn't attack.

Once you've released your fear, love will indeed cast it out. It's not a one-time, overnight, magic process. But it's true that as long as we stay committed to exposing and releasing fear, love will always be there to cast it out. God loves you enough to replace your fear with his love. Love yourself enough to release the fear, and trust the love to push fear far from the center of your motivations.

Chapter 23

When the Executions Begin

I 'll admit, when I hear the word 'executive', I don't think 'execute'. I think 'executioner'.

I grew up in the '70's and '80's, when kicking butt and taking names were the silver screen signs of a strong leader. Who didn't love Dirty Harry and Rambo, and Reagan when he said, "Mr. Gorbachev, open this gate. Mr. Gorbachev, tear down this wall!"?

Do you remember all of Dirty Harry and Rambo's friends, and their wives? Weren't they great? I don't remember them either. They didn't exist. Hollywood knows we all realize these types can't actually succeed in anything that requires an intimate relationship. They are not leaders. They fly solo.

Reagan is the obvious exception. Although I didn't have the privilege of meeting him in person, I imagine that, like Archie and Simon, he'd already met his Tim by the time he took the reigns of the country. Being strong is not in any way opposed to leading in the pasture – remember that leaders defend those they love.

But being an executioner is opposed to leading like the Good Shepherd.

So what do we do when our leader is an executioner? What happens if we find ourselves in a job or a marriage with someone who runs around slicing throats?

This is an extremely tough situation, and there is no single, simple solution to the dilemma.

It may help you to realize that most executioners are driven around, at breakneck speed, by their elephants. Their antics are usually controlled by their unrealized underlying fears, not by humility, understanding, or awareness. They don't like being driven by their fears any more than you like living with the consequences thereof.

If you love an executioner, whether it's your boss or pastor or spouse, understand they often need a Tim to come alongside of them. The problem is most executioners don't go looking for a Tim. However, there is hope – once their elephant has slammed them into one too many trees, the trauma from that pain usually sends them seeking their Tim.

The worst thing you can do for the executioner you love is to shield and insulate them from the painful natural consequences of their rampaging elephant (which is fully them – don't excuse the behavior by saying it's not). Standing by and absorbing the brunt of the rampaging elephant is not loving. It's not loving toward them, it's not loving toward yourself, and it's not loving toward the world they live in. Stop trying to be a buffer between the executioner and the outcomes that arise from their actions. Loving them requires that you let them see, experience, and feel the result of getting smashed into their wall.

And remember, there is no church, job, or marriage that you cannot excuse yourself from, even if only for long enough to let your executioner discover their Tim and grow up.

Chapter 24

When the Temperature Rises

Any time more than two people share the same space, the temperature will rise. This is not abnormal. However, it's imperative that you not let the temperature rise to the ignition point. A leader knows emotions, and knows the temperature of those he loves.

In the story of Ted and Gail, her temperature rose until she exploded. Ted could have left Gail, or, if she was willing, he could have drugged her into zombieland. But Ted chose a higher path – he chose to listen to the advice of Tim, who showed Ted that Ted himself was both the cause and solution to his wife's rising temperature.

When we have a repeated pattern of those we lead overheating, we can be fairly confident it's related to one of three things: our lack of understanding (which includes listening and empathy), our lack of awareness (which includes connecting to a problem and seeing it from all angles), or our lack of humility (which includes eliminating defensiveness). So let's start there; I think you'll be surprised with how these three traits cool an overheated room.

When we have an overheating spouse, the first key is to work on yourself. Follow the model of the Good Shepherd to learn how successful relationships work. Tim knew the Good Shepherd way of leading, but he clarified it even further for Ted: he told him three ways to be proactive, instead of reactive.

First, he told Ted to observe. When Gail's temperature was on the rise, it didn't come out in her words. Words didn't come until she'd ignited. But her temperature did come out in her facial expressions and body language. Ted had to become a student of this. When he saw the signs, it was his cue to step in and invite her to open up to him. This is not just a solution for those who are prone to ignition, this is a prescription for all loving relationships. I've heard men complain that their wife expects them to read their mind, but in reality he can look a few inches lower – her face often shows him exactly what she's feeling. But we miss it. This is worth intentional, focused study. My own grandparents, who'd been married seventy-five years, could look across the room at each other and write a paragraph on what the other was feeling in that moment. Studying your partner is not just about a relief valve, it's an essential component of true intimacy.

Second, Tim instructed Ted to talk. It wasn't as much about talking as it was removing the barriers and distractions to communication, and to honestly and authentically listen. People rarely boil over when they feel heard, as is taught to every member of the customer complaint department. People yearn to be heard and understood, and it's natural for our temperature to rise when we are trying to express ourselves and the person on the other end just doesn't get it. In talking, Tim advised Ted to avoid two things: defensiveness, and quick solutions. When the listener goes to these places, they're not actually listening – they've moved on. This is exasperating, and a sure fire way to turn up the heat. It's not love – remember, exasperating is on the *love isn't* list. Verbal communication happens when the speaker is speaking and the listener is listening. Anything short of that can't really be called communication.

Third, Tim suggested that Ted be intentional about relaxation. This is a must for any relationship, whether work, church, or family. We are designed to work in cycles. Just like we can't stay awake forever, we can't stay wound up forever. We are designed to wind up and wind down, and there must be room for both. Companies find that when they facilitate winding down, workers are more productive and more connected to each other. The same is true at church and at home.

Tim had three ideas for Ted to facilitate relaxation for Gail. He started with the idea of a vacation. This is a time to fully unwind, to get away from all regular responsibilities and duties and simply 'be' together. He continued with the idea of weekend getaways. These don't have to be big, but they have to break up the monotony and predictability of the regular cycle. The Hebrews accomplished this with Shabbat, a day where everything was changed up, and an annual Seder, a night that was different from all the others (among other parties!). Last, Tim recommended relieving some of the expected burden of daily life. Married people would be wise to find one thing each day that their spouse was expecting to have to do, and do it for them. Ted hired a housekeeper, Martha organized Archie's ties. Loading the dishwasher, fueling the car, or ordering take-out can go miles in helping your spouse relax. Do something every day that helps someone you love be a little less burdened.

Remember that thing that love isn't? It isn't thoughtless, it isn't inattentive, and it isn't burdensome.

Chapter 25

Recognizing the Ultimate Leader in the Pasture

Joshua Bar-Joseph, who today we call Jesus Christ, set the ultimate example of leading with love.

As a newborn, he slept in a livestock feeding trough instead of a crib. He was baptized by a wild hillbilly in a dirty river, not by a minister in a church tank. He'd sometimes sleep in the open air, or on a filthy fishing boat. Trained as a construction worker, he had a clear career path, but chose to wander the countryside delivering his message of leading with love – often relying on the generosity of thieves and children for his lunch. His hands were rough, his skin was dark, and his feet were dirty.

He embraced those whom the church excluded. While the church service was in session, he could be found out partying. As the minister watched, he violated the sacred and cardinal rules of his denomination. When the elders confronted him, he told them in no uncertain terms that they misinterpreted scripture, and that their evangelistic efforts were driving people to hell.

There was nothing about his life that hinted at his future epitaph: "Joshua from Nazareth – The King of God's Chosen".

But Jesus Christ led with love. In fact, he was audacious enough to tell a distinguished theologian that the six hundred and thirteen laws defining right relationship with God and mankind could be summarized into two rules: Love God, and everyone else, too.

In his stories and journeys, he would show people who to love: criminals, those who used their sexuality differently, members of the unaccepted race, low-class immigrants, and people who didn't qualify for church membership – among others.

He was unabashed and unashamed when he said the will of God boiled down to living life this way.

He didn't hold an office, even though his epitaph rightly declared him king. He didn't write a book, although tens of thousands of books were written about him. And he didn't start a religion, but the majority of religious people today point back to him as their inspiration.

We can learn a lot from the life of Jesus. My final word of advice is as much for me as it is for you:

Today,

let's get into the pasture

and lead with love.

About the Author

Nigel Davidoff is a father, businessman, and voyager through this wonderful life. He is a pioneer of early Internet technologies and has manned the helm of the same company for twenty years. He spends his leisure time riding motorcycles, flying airplanes, and relishing the beauty of God's gorgeous underwater creation around the world as a master scuba diver. In his second half of life, Nigel is eager to contribute to the cures for diabetes and cancer.

Nigel can be reached at pasture@nigeldavidoff.com.